M000102499

201 Interview Questions

SAP Finance and Controlling

Copyright @ 2006 by Genieholdings.com, Inc.

Published 2006 by Genie Press a division of Genieholdings.com, Inc.

All rights reserved. No part of this publication may be used or reproduced in any manner whatsoever without either the prior written permission of the publisher or a license permitting restricted copying in the United States or abroad.

Printed by Lightning Source

ISBN 0-9777251-1-1

Cover Design	: Heila Rowan & Elaine Lanmon
Technical Editor	: Kevin Wilson
Copy Editor	: Erland Otte
Book Formatting & Layout Design	: Kerry Wilson

Please visit www.Genieholdings.com with any comments or questions.

Trademarks

Trademarked na mes may appear in this book. Rather than use a trademark symbol with every occurrence of a trademarked name, we use the names only in an editorial fashion and to the benefit of the trademark owner, with no intention of infringement of the trademark.

SAP, SAP Logo, R/3, mySAP, mySAP.com and other SAP products and services mentioned herein are trademarks or registered trademarks of SAP AG.

All product names are trademarks of their respective companies.

Disclaimer

This is not a product of SAP AG nor are they the publisher of this book and are not responsible for it under any aspect of the law. This publication is an independent view and is for instructional purposes only. The publisher does not offer any warranties or representations nor does it accept any liabilities with respect to the content of this publication. The information in this book is distributed on an "as is" basis, without warranty. Although every precaution has been taken in the preparation of this work, neither the author(s), nor Genie Press of Genieholdings.com Inc. shall have any liability to any person or entity with respect to any loss or damage caused or alleged to be caused directly or indirectly by the information contained in this work.

201 Interview Questions

SAP Finance and Controlling

by A Vishwanath

Genie Press
http://www.geniepress.com

TABLE OF CONTENTS

<u>FOREWORD</u>

"Vish and I have had a long, successful path over the years that we have worked together. I admire his knowledge, drive and most of all his honesty and integrity. He has proven knowledge and skills in the FICO area, highlighted by his enormously successful FICO configuration pack, made available through various sales channels, including Genieholdings.com. Thus, I can attest first hand, that he is the "real deal" when it comes to FICO. If you're looking for a FICO related job, then sharpen up your skills with this book... if you're looking to find a sharp FICO consultant but don't know what to ask, start reading!

Through Genieholdings.COM and Genie Press we are striving towards bringing REAL value to SAP interested parties. I trust that you will enjoy this book and it's bonus material."

Kevin Wilson – Co-Founder, Genieholdings.COM

<u>INTRODUCTION</u>

How to use this book:

<u>As a consultant / analyst:</u>

- ✔ Start by reading from cover to cover.
- ✔ Repeat until you think you know all the details.
- ✔ Now practice what you have learnt in the system.

<u>If you are an employer looking to hire/contract a FICO professional:</u>

- ✔ The first part of the book highlights key questions that you should be able to ask a candidate and gauge their competency.

- ✔ By randomly adding a few questions from the rest of the book, you can focus on a specific area and ensure that the candidate is compentent in the relevant information.

- ✔ Before interviewing a candidate, make sure that you fully understand the question and answer. Every effort has been made to ensure that the questions and answers are simple in their explanations but you may need to revise some of them before an interview.

- ✔ We suggest highlighting those questions that you wish to ask, familiarizing yourself with the answers and then conducting the interview.

You will notice that the chapter and topic that is being covered is always listed on the top of each page. This is to remind you of the context of the question being asked to ensure that the candidate can respond as appropriately as possible. For example, if you are asking a General Ledger question then explain to the candidate that the following question pertains to the General Ledger.

Key:

Each question has a rating which is illustrated by the following symbols:

①	Basic
①②	Intermediate
①②③	Expert

As an added benefit we have provided several worksheets and bonus material on Geniepress.com. This includes candidate worksheets, which have the questions marked out as well as providing space for the candidate name, the date of the interview and their overall scores.

To access this information:
- ✔ Go to http://www.geniepress.com/201fico
- ✔ Enter the username 201fico and password F1C201

Good luck and enjoy!

Key Questions

These are the top questions,

to ask of a consultant,

to gauge their competency level

in a fast and efficient manner.

Basic

1. **What is a Company Code and what are the basic organizational assignments to a company code?** ①

    A Company Code is a legal entity for which financial statements such as a Profit and Loss statement and a Balance Sheet are generated.

    The basic organizational assignments to a Company Code are :
    - Plant
    - Purchasing Organization
    - Sales Organization.

2. **How many "Chart of Accounts" can a Company code have?** ①

    A Company code can have only one Chart of Accounts assigned to it, called the Operational Chart of Accounts.

    The Chart of Accounts is simply a list of General Ledger Accounts.

    SAP also provides an option of mapping two additional Chart of Accounts to a Company Code ie.:
    - Country Chart of Accounts.
    - Group Chart of Accounts.

    These assignments are not mandatory.

3. **Explain the importance of the GR/IR clearing account.** ①

    GR/IR is an interim account. In the legacy system of a client, if the goods are received and the invoice is not received, the provision is made for the same.

In SAP, at the Goods receipt stage, the system passes an accounting entry - debiting the Inventory and crediting the GR/IR Account.

Subsequently, when an invoice is received, the GR/IR account is debited and the Vendor account is credited. That way, till the time that the invoice is not received, the GR/IR is shown as uncleared items.

4. Where do the characteristics in Profitability Analysis come from? ①

The characteristics that are defined above, basically come from either the Customer Master or the Material Master.

5. What is the difference between Profitability analysis and Profit center accounting? ①

Profitability analysis lets you analyze the profitability of segments of your market according to:
- Products
- Customers
- Regions
- Divisions

It provides your sales, marketing, planning and management organizations with decision support from a market oriented viewpoint.

Profit center accounting lets you analyze profit and loss for profit centers. It makes it possible to evaluate different areas or units within your company.

Profit center accounting can be structured according to:
- Region
- Plants
- Functions
- Products (product ranges)

6. Explain the organizational assignment in the controlling module? ①

Company codes are assigned to the controlling area. A Controlling Area is assigned to the operating concern.

Controlling Area is the umbrella under which all controlling activities of Cost Center Accounting, Product costing, Profitability Analysis and Profit Center are stored.

Operating Concern is the highest node in Profitability Analysis.

7. What is primary and secondary cost element? ①

Every Profit and Loss GL account, that needs to be controlled, has to be defined as a cost element in SAP. Just as in FI, General Ledger Accounts exist, in Controlling we have cost element.

Each FI General Ledger Account that is a Profit and Loss Account is also created as a cost element in SAP.

✔ **Primary Cost Elements**

Those which are created from FI general Ledger Accounts and impact the financial accounts.

For example, traveling expenses, consumption account and in fact, any Profit and Loss GL account.

✔ **Secondary Cost Elements**

Those which are created only in controlling and do not affect the financials of the company. They are used for internal reporting only. The postings to these accounts do not affect the profit or loss of the company.

The following categories exist for secondary cost elements:

21 Internal Settlements

Cost elements of this category are used to settle order costs to objects in controlling. For example, cost centers and pa segments.

31 Order/Results Analysis

Used to calculate WIP on the order/project.

41 Overheads

Used to calculate indirect costs from cost centers to orders.

42 Assessment

Used to calculate costs during assessment.

43 Internal Activity Allocations

Used to allocate costs during internal activity allocation. For example, machine labor.

8. What configuration settings are maintained in the costing variant? ①

Costing variant forms the link between the application and customizing, since all cost estimates are carried out and saved with reference to a costing variant.

The costing variant contains all the control parameters for costing.

The configuration parameters are maintained for:

- ✔ Costing type
- ✔ Valuation variants
- ✔ Date control
- ✔ Quantity structure control.

In costing type we specify which material master field should be updated.

In valuation variant we specify the following:

- ✔ The sequence or order the system should go about for accessing prices for the material master (planned price, standard price, moving average price etc).

- ✔ It also contains which price should be considered for activity price calculation.

- ✔ How the system should select BOM and routing.

Intermediate

9. What is a settlement profile and why is it needed? ① ②

All the costs or revenues that are collected in the Production order or Sales order, for example, have to be settled to a receiver at the end of the period.

This receiver could be a Gl account, a cost center, profitability analysis or asset.

In order to settle the costs of the production order or sales order a settlement profile is needed.

In a settlement profile you define a range of control parameters for settlement. You must define the settlement profile before you can enter a settlement rule for a sender.

The Settlement Profile is maintained in the Order Type and defaults during creation of the order.

Settlement profile includes:

- ✔ The retention period for the settlement documents.
- ✔ Valid receivers GL account, cost center, order, WBS element, fixed asset, material, profitability segment, sales order, cost objects, order items, business process.
- ✔ Document type is also attached here.
- ✔ Allocation structure and PA transfer structure is also attached to the settlement profile for example, A1.

The settlement profile created is then attached to the order type.

10. **How are essential characteristics defined in the Profitability analysis module?** ① ②

Several essential characteristics (like sales organization and customer, product) are predefined automatically for every operating concern. These are known as fixed characteristics.

In addition to fixed characteristics up to 50 non-fixed characteristics can be added to an operating concern. These non-fixed characteristics must be added to the field catalog before they can be used to define a new operating concern.

11. **When a standard cost estimate is run for a finished good, does SAP calculate cost estimate for its components such as raw and packing materials?** ① ②

Yes. SAP calculates the cost estimate even for raw and packing materials and stores it in the standard price field for information purposes.

12. **How do you prevent the system from calculating the cost estimate for raw and packing materials when you run a standard cost estimate for the finished goods?** ① ②

To prevent the system from calculating cost estimates for raw and packing materials, you need to select the "No costing" checkbox in the costing view of the material master.

13. How is it possible to apply 2 different overhead rates for 2 different finished goods? ① ②

It is possible through overhead groups. You configure 2 overhead keys and the define rates for each of these overhead keys. These two overhead keys are then assigned to the two overhead groups. These overhead groups are attached in the costing view of the finished goods material master.

14. In period 1 there is a WIP (Work in Process) posted of $22,000. In period 2 further goods issues are done to the extent of $15,000. How will the system calculate WIP for period 2? ① ②

The system will post a delta WIP of $15,000 in period 2.

15. Which is the Result analysis category that is normally maintained for the WIP (Work in Process) calculation? ① ②

The result analysis category, WIPR. Work in process with requiremnt to capitalize costs is normally maintained for WIP calculation.

16. What is the meaning of additive costs in SAP and why is it required? ① ②

Additive costs are used to add costs manually, to a material cost estimate, when it cannot be calculated by the system.

Examples of such costs are freight charges, insurance costs and stock transfer costs.

17. What is the configuration required for additive costs? ① ②

To include additive costs in the material cost estimate, you need to set the indicator "Incl. additive costs" for each valuation strategy in the valuation variant.

Further, you also need to set in the costing variant to include additive costs.

18. What configuration settings are available, to set up valuation, using material cost estimate, in costing based profitability analysis? ① ②

In costing based profitability analysis you define costing keys.

A costing key is a set of access parameters, which are used in valuation, to determine which data in Product cost planning should be read.

In the costing key you attach the costing variant and specify whether the system should read:

- ✔ The current standard cost estimate,
- ✔ The previous standard cost estimate,
- ✔ The future standard cost estimate or
- ✔ A saved cost estimate.

The configuration settings to determine this costing key is as follows:

- ✔ Assign costing keys to the products. Three costing keys can be attached to a single product for a specific point of valuation, record type and plan version.
- ✔ Assign costing keys to Material types.

✔ Assign costing keys to any characteristics. You can use your own strategy to determine the costing keys. This is through user defined assignment tables.

19. What are the precautions to be taken while maintaining the 3KEH table for profit center accounting? ① ②

You should not maintain the customer and vendor reconciliation accounts in the 3KEH table. Further, you should also not maintain the special GL accounts in this table since we are transferring the customer and vendor balances to the profit center module through separate month end programs. If the reconciliation's accounts are maintained here, it will result in double posting in the profit center module.

20. There exist 2 production versions for a finished product. Which production version will the system pick up while calculating the standard cost estimate? ① ②

The system will pick up the first version by default while calculating the standard cost estimate.

21. There exist 2 production versions for a finished product. The product cost accountant wants the second version to be selected while creating the cost estimate. How can you do that? ① ②

There are 2 options available:

✔ While creating the standard cost estimate in transaction code CK11N, you can select the Production version manually or the Bill of Material and routing.

> ✔ You lock production version 1. Create a copy of production version 1 and name it as production version 2. The system will now access production version 2 as the first version.

22. What is done by the GR/IR regrouping program? ① ②

The balance in a GR/IR account is basically because of 2 main types of transactions:

✔ **Goods delivered but invoice not received**

Here the goods receipt is made but an invoice has not yet been received from the vendor. In such a scenario GR/IR account will have a credit balance.

✔ **Invoiced received but goods not delivered**

Here the invoice is received from the vendor and accounted for, but goods have not been received. In such a scenario GR/IR account will have a debit balance.

The GR/IR account would contain the net value of these two types of transactions. The GR/IR regrouping program analyses the above transactions and regroups them to the correct adjustment account.

The balance resulting from the first scenario, will be regrouped to another liability account and the balance resulting from the second scenario, will be regrouped to an asset account.

23. How do you keep the FI posting period open for only certain GL codes? ① ②

In transaction code OB52, click on new entries and maintain an interval or single GL code for the account type S, with the posting period variant.

If the GL codes are not in sequence then you need to maintain further entries for the posting period variant and account type S.

24. When you create the customer and vendor number range, is it created for a company code? ① ②

No. The customer and vendor number range are created at the client level without reference to any company code. Any company code can use the customer and vendor code by creating the company code view.

25. Which is the payment term that gets defaulted when the transaction is posted for the customer (accounting view or the sales view)? ① ②

The payment term in the accounting view of the customer master comes into picture if the transaction originates from the FI module. If an FI invoice is posted (FB70) to the customer, then the payment terms are defaulted from the accounting view of the customer master.

The payment term in the sales view of the customer master comes into picture if the transaction originates from the SD module. A sales order is created in the SD module. The payment terms are defaulted in the sales order from the sales view of the customer master.

26. There is a production order with an order quantity of 1000 kgs. During the month 500 kgs of goods were produced. What will be the system treatment at the month end? ① ②

The system will first check the status of the production order. Since the status of the order is not DLV (delivered) it will calculate a WIP for the production order.

27. How do you go about configuring the material ledger? ① ②

- Activate Valuation Areas for the Material Ledger.
- Assign Currency Types to the Material Ledger Type.
- Assign Material Ledger Types to Valuation Areas.
- Maintain Number Ranges for Material Ledger Documents.
- Activate Actual costing (whether activity update relevant for price determination).
- Activate Actual cost component split.
- Customizing settings in OBYC.

28. How is Bank Reconciliation handled in SAP? ① ②

Bank reconciliation typically follows the procedure below:

- First, the payment made to a Vendor is posted to an interim bank clearing account.
- Subsequently, while performing reconciliation, an entry is posted to the Main Bank account.
- Similarly, the checks received from a customer are posted to an interim bank clearing account (check incoming account).
- The checks cleared are updated to the Main bank account when the bank statement is uploaded (either manually or electronically).

You can perform a bank reconciliation either manually or electronically.

29. How do you go about setting the FI MM account determination? ① ②

FI MM settings are maintained in transaction code OBYC. Within these there are various transaction keys to be maintained, for example, BSX, WRX, GBB, PRD. These transactions keys are called when material movements are performed in Material Management.

For each of the transaction keys, you need to select rules for which you will be maintaining details.

For example, Transaction key BSX (For inventory balance sheet accounts):

- ✓ The rules you can select are valuation modification or valuation class.
- ✓ Valuation modification is required if you want to maintain plant wise different GL codes.

After saving the rule, you maintain the GL code for the combination of valuation modification and valuation class.

For example, Transaction key GBB (offsetting account for inventory postings generally goods issue/scrapping/ delivery of goods etc). Here you maintain the rules:

- ✓ Debit/credit
- ✓ General modification
- ✓ Valuation modification
- ✓ Valuation class

The GL account is maintained for the above combination.

Expert

30. Is it possible to maintain plant wise different GL codes? ① ② ③

Yes. To be able to do so the valuation grouping code should be activated.

The valuation grouping code is maintained per plant and is configured in the MM module. Account codes should be maintained per valuation grouping code, after doing this configuration.

31. What are the problems faced when a Business area is configured? ① ② ③

When a Business area is configured, the GL account balance needs to be balanced, per business area. This is achieved through the transaction code F.5D.

Normally all the GL accounts are split per business area but there might arise some problems while splitting the tax account balances as per business area.

32. Is it possible to configure the system to pick up a different exchange rate type, for a particular transaction? ① ② ③

Yes it is possible. In the document type definition of GL, you need to attach a different exchange rate type.

33. How do you maintain the number range in a Production environment? Do you create it directly in the Production system or do you do it by means of transport? ①②③

Number range is to be created in the production client. You can transport it by way of a transport request but creating it directly in the production client is more advisable and common practice.

34. How do you configure the automatic payment program? ①②③

The following are the steps for configuring the automatic payment program:

Step 1 - set up the following:

- ✔ Company code for Payment transaction.
- ✔ Define sending and paying company code.
- ✔ Tolerance days for payable.
- ✔ Minimum % for cash discount.
- ✔ Maximum cash discount.
- ✔ Special GL transactions to be paid.

Step 2 - set up the following:

- ✔ Paying company code for payment transaction.
- ✔ Minimum amount for outgoing payment.
- ✔ No exchange rate diff.
- ✔ Separate payment for each ref.
- ✔ Bill/exchange payment.
- ✔ Form for payment advice.

Step 3 - set up the following:

- Payment method per country.
- Whether Outgoing payment.
- Check or bank transfer or B/E.
- Whether allowed for personnel payment.
- Required master data.
- Document types.
- Payment medium programs.
- Currencies allowed.

Step 4 - set up the following:

- Payment method per company code for payment transactions.
- Set up per payment method and company code.
- The minimum and maximum amount.
- Whether payment per due day.
- Bank optimization by bank group or by postal code or no optimization.
- Whether Foreign currency allowed.
- Customer/Vendor bank abroad allowed.
- Attach the payment form check.
- Whether payment advice required.

Step 5 - set up the following:

- Bank Determination for Payment Transactions.
- Rank the house banks as per the following:

    Payment method

    Currency

    Give them ranking numbers
- Set up house bank sub account (GL code).
- Available amounts for each bank.

✔ House bank, account ID, currency and available amount.

✔ Value date specification.

35. Where do you attach the check payment form? ① ② ③

It is attached to the payment method per company code.

36. How are Tolerances for Invoice verification defined? ① ② ③

The following are instances of tolerances that can be defined for Logistic Invoice Verification:

✔ Small Differences.

✔ Moving Average Price variances.

✔ Quantity variances.

✔ Price variances.

Based on the client requirement, the transaction can be "Blocked" or Posted with a "Warning" in the event of the Tolerances being exceeded.

Tolerances are nothing but the difference between invoice amount and payment amount or difference between goods receipt amount and invoice amount which is acceptable to the client.

37. How do you configure check deposit? ① ② ③

The following are the steps for configuring check deposit:

✔ Create account symbols for the main bank and incoming check account.

✔ Assign accounts to account symbols.

✔ Create keys for posting rules.

- ✔ Define posting rules.
- ✔ Create business transactions and assign posting rule.
- ✔ Define variant for check deposit.

38. How do you configure a manual bank statement? ① ② ③

The following are the steps for configuring a manual bank statement:

- ✔ Create account symbols for the main bank and sub accounts.
- ✔ Assign accounts to account symbols.
- ✔ Create keys for posting rules.
- ✔ Define posting rules.
- ✔ Create a business transaction and assign a posting rule.
- ✔ Define a variant for the manual bank statement.

39. How do you configure an electronic bank statement? ① ② ③

The steps for configuring an electronic bank statement are the same as for a manual bank statement except for the additional steps which you will see down below.

- ✔ Create account symbols for the main bank and sub accounts.
- ✔ Assign accounts to account symbols.
- ✔ Create keys for posting rules.
- ✔ Define posting rules.
- ✔ Create transaction type.
- ✔ Assign external transaction type to posting rules.
- ✔ Assign Bank accounts to transaction types.

40. What are the special steps and care to be taken in Fixed Asset data migration into the SAP system, especially when Profit center accounting is active? ① ② ③

Data migration is slightly different from a normal transaction which happens in the asset accounting module:

- ✔ Normal asset transactions, like asset acquisition retirements, update the asset master and automatically update the asset GL account at the same time. In Asset Migration the asset master is updated with values through a transaction code called as AS91. The values updated on the master are Opening Gross value and the accumulated depreciation. The reconciliation GL account is not automatically updated at this point of time.

- ✔ The reconciliation accounts (GL codes) are updated manually through another transaction code called as OASV.

- ✔ If profit center is active, then after uploading assets through AS91 you should transfer the asset balances to profit center accounting through a transaction called 1KEI.

- ✔ Thereafter you remove the Asset GL code (reconciliation accounts) from the 3KEH table for PCA and update the Asset reconciliation account (GL code) through OASV.

- ✔ After this step, you again update the Asset reconciliation account in the 3KEH table.

The reason you remove the Asset reconciliation code from 3KEH table is that double posting will happen to PCA if you update the Asset reconciliation manually.

41. Is it possible to have depreciation calculated to the day? ① ② ③

Yes it is possible. You need to switch on the indicator "Dep to the day" in the depreciation key configuration.

42. How do you go about configuring for the sales order costing? ① ② ③

The flow is as follows:

Sales order ➔ Requirement Type➔ Requirement Class ➔ All settings for controlling.

In a sales order you have a requirement type. In configuration, the requirement Class is attached to the requirement type and in this requirement class all configuration settings are maintained for controlling.

In the requirement class we attach the costing variant. We attach the condition type EK02 where we want the sales order cost to be updated, and the account assignment category. In the account assignment category we define whether the sales order will carry cost or not. In case we do not want to carry cost on the sales order, we keep the consumption posting field blank.

Here we define the Results Analysis version which helps to calculate the Results Analysis for the Sales order if required.

43. **There are 2 plants in a company code. First plant is the manufacturing plant and another plant is the selling plant. Finished goods are manufactured at the manufacturing plant and transferred to the selling plant. How is standard cost estimate calculated at the selling plant given the fact that the cost at both the plants should be the same?** ①②③

The special procurement type needs to be configured which specifies in which plant the system is to look up for cost. Here a special procurement key specifying plant 1 (manufacturing plant) should be configured.

This special procurement type must be entered in the costing view or the MRP view of the finished good material master record in plant 2.

When you cost the finished good at plant 2, the system will transfer the standard cost estimate from plant 1 to plant 2.

44. **What configuration needs to done for using Mixed costing?** ①②③

Quantity Structure type for mixed costing must be configured. Here we specify the time dependency of the structure type. The following options exist:

- ✔ You have no time dependency.
- ✔ It is based on the fiscal year.
- ✔ It is based on a fixed time period.

This quantity structure type is then assigned to the costing version.

45. There are Result analysis categories in WIP (Work in Process). What does the result analysis category Reserves for unrealized costs mean? ① ② ③

If you are calculating the work in process at actual costs, the system will create reserves for unrealized costs, if the credit for the production order based on goods receipts is greater than the debit of the order with actual costs incurred. The Result analysis category RUCR (Reserves for unrealized cost) would need to be maintained. This is not normally maintained in most companies.

46. How do you configure split valuation? ① ② ③

The configuration steps involved in split valuation are:

- ✔ Activate split valuation – Configure whether split valuation is allowed for the company code.

- ✔ Determine the valuation categories and valuation types that are allowed for all valuation areas.

- ✔ Allocate the valuation types to the valuation categories.

- ✔ Determine the local valuation categories for each valuation area and activate the categories to be used in your valuation area.

47. What are the steps involved before you run a cost estimate for a split valuated material? ① ② ③

- ✔ Create procurement alternatives based on the valuation types for the material.

- ✔ Maintain Mixing ratios for the procurement alternatives.

48. **What is the basic difference in WIP calculation in product cost by order versus product cost by period (repetitive manufacturing)?** ① ② ③

Generally in product cost by order, WIP is calculated at actual costs and in product cost by period WIP is calculated at target costs.

49. **What are the problems faced when a material ledger is activated?** ① ② ③

When a material ledger is activated it is imperative that actual costing run is done every month. Actual costing run needs to be done immediately after the new month roll over. After the actual costing run you cannot post any MM(Materials Management) entry to the previous period.

50. **What are the steps to be taken before you execute an actual costing run?** ① ② ③

- Execute all the allocation cycles in the cost center accounting module.
- Execute actual activity price calculation.
- Revalue all the production orders with the actual activity prices. The under or over absorbed cost on cost centers are passed on to the production order through this step of revaluation of production orders.
- Calculate overheads, do a variance calculation and finally settle the production order.
- Execute the actual costing run.

51. What are the advantages and disadvantages of Account based profitability analysis versus costing based profitability analysis? ① ② ③

The advantage of Account based PA is that it is permanently reconciled with Financial accounting.

The disadvantages are that it is not powerful as the costing based PA, since it uses accounts to get values. No Contribution margin planning can be done since it cannot access the standard cost estimate. Further no variance analysis is readily available.

The advantages of the Costing based PA are manifold:

- ✔ Greater Reporting capabilities since many characteristics are available for analysis.

- ✔ This form of PA accesses the Standard cost estimate of the manufactured product and gives a split according to the cost component split (from the product costing module) when the bills are posted.

- ✔ Contribution margin can be planned in this module since the system automatically accesses the standard cost estimate of the product based on the valuation approaches.

- ✔ Variance analysis is readily available here since the variance categories can be individually mapped to the value fields.

Disadvantage:

- ✔ Since it uses a costing based approach, sometimes it does not reconcile with financial accounting.

52. Can both Account based and Costing based Profitability analysis be configured at the same time? ① ② ③

Yes. It is possible to configure both types of costing based profitability analysis at the same time.

53. Is there any additional configuration required for Account based profitability analysis as compared to costing based profitability analysis? ① ② ③

No. There are no special configurations required except for activating the account based profitability analysis while maintaining the operating concern.

40

CHAPTER 1

Enterprise Structure

Enterprise Structure

1. **What is a Company Code and what are the basic organizational assignments to a company code?** ①

   A Company Code is a legal entity for which financial statements such as Profit and Loss and Balance Sheets are generated. The basic organizational assignments to a Company Code are:
   - Plant
   - Purchasing Organization
   - Sales Organization.

2. **What is the relationship between a Controlling Area and a Company Code?** ①

   A Controlling Area can have 2 types of relationship with a Company Code:
   - Single Controlling Area → Single Company Code
   - Single Controlling Area → Cross Company Codes/ Multiple Company Codes

   Controlling can have a one- to-one relationship or a one-to-many relationship with different company codes.

   A Controlling Area is the topmost organizational element under which all controlling (or Internal Accounting) activities of Cost Center Accounting, Product Costing, Profit Center and Profitability Analysis are stored.

   In a similar way the Company Code is the topmost organizational element for Financial Accounting eg. GL, AR, AP and Asset Accounting.

3. How many "Chart of Accounts" can a Company code have? ①

A Company code can have only one Chart of Accounts assigned to it, called the Operational Chart of Accounts. The Chart of Accounts is nothing but the list of General Ledger Accounts.

SAP also provides an option of mapping two additional Chart of Accounts to a Company Code:

- ✔ Country Chart of Accounts and
- ✔ Group Chart of Accounts.

These two assignments are not mandatory.

4. What are the options in SAP when it comes to fiscal years? ①

A fiscal year is nothing but the way financial data is stored in the system. SAP provides you with the combination of 12 normal periods and also four special periods. These periods are stored in what is called the fiscal year variant.

There are two types of Fiscal Year Variants

- ✔ Calendar Year e.g. Jan-Dec
- ✔ Year Dependent Fiscal Year.

5. What is a year dependent fiscal year variant? ① ②

In a year dependent fiscal year variant the number of days in a month are not as per the calendar month. For example, for the year 2005 the period January ends on the 29th, February ends on the 27th and March ends on the 29th . For the year 2006, January ends on the 30th, February ends on the 26th and March ends on the 30th.

This is applicable to many countries especially USA. Every year this fiscal year variant needs to be configured to correspond to the Financial Periods of the business.

6. How does posting happen in MM (Materials Management) during special periods? ① ②

There are no postings that happen from MM in special periods. Special periods are only applicable to the FI module. They are required for making any additional postings such as closing entries, provisions etc. that happen during the quarter end or year end.

7. How many currencies can be configured for a company code? ① ② ③

A Company Code can have 3 currencies. They are:

- ✔ Local currency i.e. company code currency and
- ✔ 2 Parallel currencies.

This gives the company the flexibility to report in different currencies.

8. For parallel currencies do you need to configure an additional ledger? ① ② ③

Where only 2 currencies are configured (Company code currency and a parallel currency) there is no need for an additional ledger. In case the third parallel currency is configured and if it is different than the second currency type, you would then need to configure an additional ledger.

9. **If there are two company codes with different Chart of Accounts, how can you consolidate their activities?**
    ①②③

> In this case you would either need to write an ABAP program or you would need to implement the Special Consolidation Module of SAP. If both the company codes use the same Chart of Accounts then standard SAP reports give you the consolidated figure.

CHAPTER 2

Finance

FI-GL

10. Give some examples of GL accounts that should be posted automatically through the system and how this is defined in the system. ① ②

Stock and Consumption accounts are instances of GL accounts that should be automatically posted. In the GL account master record, a check box exists wherein the automatic posting option is selected called "Post Automatically Only".

11. What is an Account group and where is it used? ①

Account groups exist for the definition of a GL account, Vendor and Customer master records.

An Account Group controls:

✔ The Number Ranges for the creation of the Master Data i.e. it determines the number that is assigned to a master record (GL, Vendor or Customer) on creation.

✔ It controls the field status of the Company Code View of the Master Data. Based on the Account Group that is selected, it will determine & control the fields maintained at the company code level of the master data record.

12. What is a field status group? ①

Field status groups control the fields that come up during document entry. There are 4 options for field selection.

They are:
- ✔ Suppressed
- ✔ Display
- ✔ Required
- ✔ Optional

During document entry, based on the field status group, the system can control user entry, i.e. either the system can:
- ✔ Suppress the field (not visible during entry), or
- ✔ Have only a display (no user entry), or
- ✔ Make it required (in which case the user is forced to enter a value in the field), or
- ✔ Optional.

The field status group is stored in the FI GL Master Record.

13. What is the purpose of a "Document type" in SAP? ①

A Document type is specified at the Header level during transaction entry and serves the following purposes:
- ✔ It defines the Number range for documents.
- ✔ It controls the type of accounts that can be posted to e.g. Assets, Vendor, Customer, Normal GL account.
- ✔ Document type to be used for reversal of entries.
- ✔ Determines whether it can be used only for Batch input sessions.

A Document Type is created for differentiating business transactions. For example, Vendor Invoice, Credit Memo, Accrual Entries, Customer Invoice. It is a two-digit character string.

14. What is a Financial Statement Version? ①

A FSV (Financial Statement Version) is a reporting tool and can be used to depict the manner in which the financial accounts such as Profit and Loss Account, Balance Sheet and the Cash Flow Statement needs to be extracted from SAP. It is freely definable. Multiple FSV's can be defined for generating the output for various external agencies such as Banks and other statutory authorities.

15. How are input and output taxes taken care of in SAP? ① ②

A tax procedure is defined for each country and tax codes are defined within this. There is flexibility to either expense out the Tax amounts or 'inventorise' the same to Stock/Inventory.

16. What are Validations and Substitutions? ① ②

Validations/Substitutions in SAP are defined for each functional area eg. FI-GL, Assets, Controlling at the following levels:

- ✔ Document level
- ✔ Line item level

These are additional tools that are provided by SAP to controland prevent user errors and ensure accurate data entry into the system. Since these are additional tools, they are not mandatory and depending on the needs of the business, they are activated accordingly.

> **NOTE : These need to be specifically activated and setting them up is a complex task. It should only be done when it is really needed. Help from the technical team is often taken to perform this complex task.**

17. Is it possible to maintain plant wise different GL accounts? ① ② ③

Yes. You are able to do so by activating the valuation grouping code. The valuation grouping code is maintained per plant and is configured in the MM module. GL Accounts should be maintained per valuation grouping code after doing this configuration.

18. Is Business Area at the company code Level? ① ②

No. Business Area is at the Client Level. What this means is that other company codes can also post to the same Business Area. You can have a Business Area cutting across multiple company codes.

19. What are the different scenarios under which a Business Area or a Profit Center may be defined? ① ② ③

This question is disputable because both Business Areas and Profit centers are created for internal reporting. Each has its own pros and cons but many companies nowadays go for Profit center as there is a feeling that business area enhancements would not be supported by SAP in future versions.

There are typical month end procedures that need to be executed for both of them and many times reconciliation might become a big issue. A typical challenge in both of them is in cases where you do not know the Business Area or Profit Center of the transaction at the time of posting.

20. What are the problems faced when a Business area is configured? ① ② ③

When a business area is configured the GL account balance needs to be balanced as per each individual business area. This is achieved through the transaction code F.5D.

Normally all the GL accounts are split as per business area. A far greater challenge usually arises when splitting the tax account balances as per business area.

21. Is it possible to default certain values for particular fields without code? For example, company code. ①

Yes, it is possible to default values for certain fields where a parameter ID is present.

- ✔ Go to the input field to which you want to make defaults.
- ✔ Press F1, and then click the technical info push button. This should open a window that displays the corresponding parameter ID (if one has been allocated to the field) in the field data section.
- ✔ Enter this parameter id using the following path on SAP Easy access screen System ➔ User profile ➔ Own data.
- ✔ Click on parameter tab, then enter the parameter id code and enter the value you want as default. Save the user settings.

Your user profile, as set up by the security team, could also be filled with default parameter values.

22. Which is the default exchange rate type that is picked up for all SAP transactions? ① ②

The default exchange rate type picked up for all SAP transactions is M (average rate)

23. Is it possible to configure the system to pick up a different exchange rate type for a particular transaction? ①②③

Yes, it is possible. In the document type definition of GL, you need to attach a different exchange rate type.

24. What are the pre-requisites for document clearing? ①

The GL Account must be identified as open item managed. Selecting the checkbox called 'Open Item Management' in the Company Code view, of the General Ledger Master Record, does this. It helps you to manage your accounts in terms of Open Items and Cleared Items. A typical example would be GR/IR Account in SAP (Goods Received/Invoice Received Account

25. Explain the importance of the GR/IR clearing account. ①

GR/IR is an interim account. In the legacy system of a client if the goods are received and the invoice is not received the provision is made for the same.

In SAP at the Goods receipt stage the system passes an accounting entry debiting the Inventory and crediting the GR/IR Account. Subsequently when an invoice is received this GR/IR account is debited and the Vendor account is credited.

That way until invoice is received the GR/IR is shown as an uncleared item.

26. How many line items are possible in one single document? ①②

The number of line items that you can accommodate in one document is 999.

27. A Finance Document usually has an assignment field. This field automatically gets populated during data entry. Where does it get its value? ① ②

This value comes from the Sort key entered in the GL master record.

28. How do you create number ranges in a Production environment? Do you directly create it in the Production system or do you do it by means of transport? ① ② ③

The number range is to be created in the production client. You can transport it also by way of request but creating it directly in the production client is more advisable.

29. In customizing, what is the relevance of "company code productive"? ① ②

Once the company code is live (real time transactions have started) this check box helps prevents accidental deletion of many programs. This check box is activated just before go live.

30. What does the GR/IR regrouping program do? ① ② ③

The balances in a GR/IR account are basically because of 2 main types of transactions:

✔ **Goods delivered but invoice not received**

Here the Goods Receipt is made but no invoice has yet been received from the vendor. In such a scenario GR/IR account will have a credit balance.

✓ **Invoiced received but goods not delivered**

Here the Invoice is received from the vendor and accounted for, but goods have not been received. In such a scenario GR/IR account will have a debit balance.

The GR/IR account would contain the net value of the above two types of transactions. The GR/IR regrouping program analyses the above transactions and regroups them to the correct adjustment account. The balance on account of the first set of transactions will be regrouped to another liability account and the balance on account of the second set of transactions will be regrouped to an asset account.

31. What functionality is available in the financial statement version? ①②③

In the financial statement version the most important functionality available is the debit credit shift. This is more important in the case of Bank overdraft accounts that can have a debit balance or a credit balance. Thus in case of a debit balance you would require the overdraft account to be shown on the Asset side. In case of a credit balance you would require the account to be shown on the Liability side.

Language selection is also another available function in the FSV. You can control the languages in which the Financial Statement is generated.

32. Is it possible to print the financial statement version on a SAPscript form? ①

Yes. It is possible to print the financial statement version on a SAPscript form.

33. How do you configure the SAPscript form financial statement version? ① ② ③

It is possible to generate a form from the financial statement version and print the financial statements on a SAPscript form. In the "customizing for financial statement version", select the FSV you created and choose Goto ➔ Generate form ➔ One column or two column form.

You can also copy the form from the standard system.

34. Is it possible to generate a financial statement form automatically? ① ② ③

Yes. It is possible to generate a form automatically.

35. Is it possible to keep the FI posting period open only for certain GL codes? ① ②

Yes. It is possible to keep open the FI posting period only for certain GL codes.

36. How do you keep the FI posting period open only for certain GL accounts? ① ② ③

In transaction code OB52 click on new entries and maintain an interval or a single GL Account for the account type S with the posting period variant.

If the GL Accounts are not in sequence then you need to maintain further entries for the posting period variant and account type S.

37. Can the posting period variant be assigned to more than 1 company code? ①

Yes, the posting period variant can be assigned to more than one company code.

Accounts Receivable and Accounts Payable

38. When you create the customer and vendor master, at what level in SAP is it created? ① ②

The customer and vendor master is initially created at the client level without reference to a company code. Subsequently any company code can use this customer and vendor master number and extend the company code view.

39. How are Vendor Invoice payments made? ①

Vendor payments can be made in the following manner:

- Manual payments without the use of any output medium such as checks etc. (F-53)

- Automatic Payment program through checks, Wire transfers, DME etc. (F110)

40. How do you configure the automatic payment program? ① ② ③

The following steps are required for configuring the automatic payment program:

Step 1 - set up the following:

- Company code for Payment transaction
- Define sending and paying company code.
- Tolerance days for payable
- Minimum % for cash discount
- Maximum cash discount
- Special GL transactions to be paid

Step 2 - set up the following:

- Paying company code for payment transaction
- Minimum amount for outgoing payment
- No exchange rate diff
- Separate payment for each ref
- Bill/exch payment
- Form for payment advice

Step 3 - set up the following:

- Payment method per country
- Whether Outgoing payment
- Check or bank transfer or B/E
- Whether allowed for personnel payment
- Required master data
- Document types
- Payment medium programs
- Currencies allowed

Step 4 - set up the following:

- Payment method per company code for payment transactions
- Set up per payment method and company code
- The minimum and maximum amount
- Whether payment per due day
- Bank optimization by bank group or by postal code or no optimization
- Whether Foreign currency allowed
- Customer/Vendor bank abroad allowed
- Attach the payment form check
- Whether payment advice required

Step 5 - set up the following:

- ✔ Bank Determination for Payment Transactions
- ✔ Rank the house banks as per the following
- ✔ Payment method or currency and give them ranking numbers
- ✔ Set up house bank sub account (GL code)
- ✔ Available amounts for each bank
- ✔ House bank, account id, currency, available amount
- ✔ Value date specification

41. Where do you attach the check payment form? ① ② ③

It is attached to the payment method per company code.

42. Where are payment terms maintained in the customer master? ① ②

Payment terms for customer master can be maintained in two places, namely in the accounting view and the sales view.

43. Which customer master payment term is defaulted when the transaction is posted for a customer (accounting view or the sales view)? ① ②

The payment term in the accounting view of the customer master comes into picture if the transaction originates from the FI module. If an FI invoice is posted (FB70) to the customer, then the payment terms are defaulted from the accounting view of the customer master.

The payment term in the sales view of the customer master comes into picture if the transaction originates from the SD module. A sales order is created in the SD module. The payment terms are defaulted in the sales order from the sales view of the customer master.

44. Where are payment terms for the vendor master maintained? ①

Payment terms for vendor master can be maintained in two places namely, accounting view and purchasing view.

45. Which vendor master payment term is defaulted in transactions using a vendor (accounting view or purchasing view)? ①

The payment term in the accounting view of the vendor master comes into picture if the transaction originates from the FI module. If an FI invoice is posted (FB60) to the Vendor, then the payment terms is defaulted from the accounting view of the vendor master.

The payment term in the purchasing view of the vendor master comes into picture if the transaction originates from the MM module. A purchase order is created in the MM module. The payment terms are defaulted in the purchase order from the purchasing view of the vendor master.

46. Explain the entire process of Invoice verification from GR to Invoice verification in SAP with accounting entries? ①

The process is as follows:

- ✔ A goods receipt, in SAP for a purchased material, is prepared referring to a purchase order.

- ✔ When the goods receipt is posted in SAP the accounting entry passed is:

> Inventory account Debit
>
> GR/IR account Credit

> A GR/IR (which is Goods Receipt/Invoice Receipt) is a provision account that provides for the liability for the purchase. The rates for the valuation of the material are picked up from the purchase order.

- ✔ When the invoice is booked in the system through Logistics invoice verification the entry passed is as follows:

> GR/IR account Debit
>
> Vendor Credit

47. How are Tolerances for Invoice verification defined? ① ② ③

The following are instances of tolerances that can be defined for Logistic Invoice Verification:

- ✔ Small Differences
- ✔ Moving Average Price variances
- ✔ Quantity variances
- ✔ Price variances

Based on the client requirement, the transaction can be "Blocked" or posted with a "Warning" in the event of the Tolerances being exceeded.

Tolerances are nothing but the differences between invoice amount and payment amount or differences between goods receipt amount and invoice amount that is acceptable to the client.

48. Can we change the reconciliation account in the vendor master? ①②③

Yes, the reconciliation account can be changed in the vendor master provided that the authority to change has been configured. You would not normally change the reconciliation account.

49. What is the impact on the old balance when the reconciliation account in the vendor master is changed? ①②③

Any change you make to the reconciliation account is prospective and not retrospective. The old items and balances do not reflect the new account; only the new transactions reflect the new account.

50. There is an advance given by the customer which lies in a special GL account indicator A. Will this advance amount be considered for the credit check? ①②③

It depends on the configuration setting in the special GL indicator A. If the "Relevant to credit limit" indicator is switched on in the Special GL indicator A, the advances will be relevant for the credit check; otherwise it will not be relevant.

51. In payment term configuration what are the options available for setting a default baseline date? ① ②

There are 4 options available:

- ✓ No default
- ✓ Posting date
- ✓ Document date
- ✓ Entry date

52. What is generally configured in the payment term as a default for baseline date? ① ②

The document date is generally configured in the payment term as a default for the base line date.

53. How do you configure a special GL indicator for a Customer? ①

You can use an existing special GL indicator ID or create a new one. After creating a special GL indicator id, update the chart of accounts and the Reconciliation account. As a last step you need to update the special GL account.

The special GL account should also be marked as a Reconciliation account. Switch on the "Relevant for credit limit" and "Commitment warning" indicators in the master record.

Bank Accounting

54. How is Bank Reconciliation handled in SAP? ① ②

Bank reconciliation typically follows the procedure shown below:

- ✔ First, the payment made to a Vendor is posted to an interim bank clearing account (or the Bank Sub Account).

- ✔ Subsequently, while performing reconciliation, an entry is posted to the Main Bank account.

- ✔ Similarly, the checks received from a customer are posted to an interim bank clearing account (check incoming account).

- ✔ The checks cleared are updated to the Main bank account when the bank statement is uploaded (either manually or electronically).

You can do bank reconciliation either manually or electronically.

55. How do you configure check deposit? ① ② ③

The following steps are required for configuring check deposit:

- ✔ Create account symbols for the main bank and incoming check account.

- ✔ Assign accounts to account symbols

- ✔ Create keys for posting rules

- ✔ Define posting rules

- ✔ Create business transactions and assign posting rule

- ✔ Define variant for check deposit

56. What is the clearing basis for check deposit? ① ②

In the variant for check deposit we need to set up the following:

✔ Fields document number (which is the invoice number)

✔ Amount

✔ Short description of the customer.

The document number and the invoice amount act as the clearing basis.

57. How do you configure a manual bank statement? ① ② ③

The following steps are required for configuring a manual bank statement:-

✔ Create account symbols for the main bank and the sub accounts

✔ Assign accounts to account symbols

✔ Create keys for posting rules

✔ Define posting rules

✔ Create business transaction and assign posting rule

✔ Define variant for Manual Bank statement

58. How do you configure an Electronic Bank Statement? ①②③

The steps for Electronic Bank Statement are the same except for a couple of additional steps as shown below:

- ✔ Create account symbols for the main bank and the sub accounts
- ✔ Assign accounts to account symbols
- ✔ Create keys for posting rules
- ✔ Define posting rules
- ✔ Create transaction type
- ✔ Assign external transaction type to posting rules
- ✔ Assign Bank accounts to Transaction types

Fixed Assets

59. What are the organizational assignments in asset accounting? ①

Chart of depreciation is the highest node in Asset Accounting and this is assigned to the company code.

Under the Chart of depreciation all the depreciation calculations are stored.

60. How do you go about configuring Asset accounting? ① ② ③

The configuration steps in brief are described as follows:

- Copy a reference chart of depreciation areas
- Assign Input Tax indicator for non-taxable acquisitions
- Assign chart of depreciation area to company code
- Specify account determination
- Define number range interval
- Define asset classes
- Define depreciation areas posting to general ledger
- Define depreciation key

61. Explain the importance of asset classes. Give examples. ①

The asset class is the main criterion for classifying assets. Every asset must be assigned to only one asset class. Examples of asset class are Plant& Machinery, Furniture & Fixtures and Computers.

The Asset Class also controls the GL Account postings in Financial Accounting. This is done by maintaining the Account Determination Key in the Asset Class based on different transactions e.g. Acquisition, Depreciation, Sale or Scrapping.

You can also specify certain control parameters and default values for depreciation calculation and other master data in each asset class.

62. How are depreciation keys defined? ① ② ③

The configuration of depreciation key is as follows:

✔ **Select the Base Method**
In the base method you specify the depreciation type and depreciation calculation method.

✔ **Select the correct period control**
Period control specifies the depreciation start date for acquisition, acquisition in the following years, retirements and transfer.

✔ **Select the correct Multilevel Method**
Here you specify whether the depreciation key is a straight-line method or a declining balance method. Here you also specify the percentage of depreciation.

✔ You select whether multiple shift depreciation is applicable.

✔ Whether scrap value is applicable.

63. **A company has its books prepared based on a Jan – Dec calendar year for reporting to its parent company. It is also required to report accounts to tax authorities based on April- March. Can assets be managed in another depreciation area based on a different fiscal year variant (Apr- Mar)?** ① ② ③

> No. The asset accounting module cannot manage differing fiscal year variant, which has a different start date (January for book depreciation and April for tax depreciation) and different end date (December for book depreciation and March for tax depreciation). In this case you would need to implement the special purpose ledger.

64. **What special steps and care need to be taken in fixed asset data migration into SAP system, especially when Profit center accounting is active?** ① ② ③

> Data migration is slightly different from a normal transaction that happens in the Asset accounting module.
>
> In asset accounting the day-to-day transactions are normally posted with values through FI bookings and at the same time the asset reconciliation is updated online in real time.
>
> In data Migration the asset master is updated with values through transaction AS91. The values updated on the asset master are Opening Gross value and the accumulated depreciation.
>
> **The reconciliation GL account is not automatically updated at this point of time.**

The reconciliation accounts (GL codes) are updated manually through transaction code OASV.

If profit center is active, then after uploading assets through AS91 you should transfer the asset balances to profit center accounting through a program.

Thereafter you remove the Asset GL code (reconciliation accounts) from the 3KEH table for PCA and update the Asset reconciliation account (GL code) through transaction OASV.

After this step you again update the Asset reconciliation account in the 3KEH table.

The reason you remove the Asset reconciliation code from 3KEH table is that double posting will happen to PCA when you update the Asset reconciliation manually.

65. Is it possible to calculate multiple shift depreciation? Is any special configuration required? ① ② ③

Yes, it is possible to calculate multiple shift depreciation in SAP for all types of depreciation except unit of production.

In the depreciation key definition select "Increase in depreciation, no increase in expired useful life".

66. How do you maintain multiple shift depreciation in the asset master? ① ② ③

The following steps are needed to maintain multiple shift depreciation:

- ✔ The variable depreciation portion as a percentage rate needs to be maintained in the detail screen of the depreciation area.

✔ The multiple shift factor needs to be maintained in the time dependent data on the asset master record. This shift factor is then multiplied by the variable portion of ordinary depreciation.

Once you have done the above the SAP system calculates the total depreciation amount as follows:

Depreciation amount = Fixed depreciation + (variable depreciation * shift factor)

67. Let's say you have changed the depreciation rates in one of the depreciation keys due to changes in legal requirements. Does the system automatically calculate the planned depreciation as per the new rate? ①②③

No, the system does not automatically calculate the planned depreciation after the change has been made. You need to run a program for recalculation of planned depreciation.

68. What are evaluation groups? ①②③

Evaluation groups are an option for classifying assets for reports or user defined match code (search code). You can configure 5 different evaluation groups. You can update these evaluation groups on the asset master record.

69. What are group assets? ①②③

The tax requirements in some countries require calculation of depreciation at a higher group or level of assets. For this purpose you can group assets together into so-called, group assets.

70. What steps need to be taken into account during a depreciation run to ensure that the integration with the general ledger works smoothly? ① ② ③

For each depreciation area and company code, specify the following:

- ✔ The frequency of posting depreciation (monthly, quarterly etc).

- ✔ CO account assignment (cost center).

- ✔ For each company code you must define a document type for automatic depreciation posting. This document type requires its own external number range.

- ✔ You also need to specify the accounts for posting. (Account determination).

Finally, to ensure consistency between Asset Accounting and Financial Accounting, you must process the batch input session created by the posting report. If you fail to process the batch input session, an error message will appear at the next posting run.

The depreciation calculation is a month end process that is run in batch. Once the batch input has run the system posts the accounting entries into Finance.

71. How do you change the fiscal year in Asset Accounting? ①

- ✔ Run the fiscal year change program, which would open new annual value fields for each asset i.e. next year.

- ✔ The earliest you can start this program is in the last posting period of the current year.

- ✔ You have to run the fiscal year change program for your whole company code.

✓ You can only process a fiscal year change in a
subsequent year if the previous year has already
been closed for business.

Take care not to confuse the fiscal year change program
with year-end closing for accounting purposes. This
fiscal year change is needed only in Asset Accounting
for various technical reasons.

72. Is it possible to have depreciation calculated to the day? ① ② ③

Yes, it is possible. You need to switch on the indicator
"Dep to the day" in the depreciation key configuration.

73. Is it possible to ensure that no capitalization be posted in subsequent years? ① ② ③

Yes, it is possible. You need to set it in the depreciation
key configuration.

74. How are Capital Work in Progress and Assets accounted for in SAP? ①

Capital WIP is referred to as Assets under
Construction in SAP and is represented by a specific
Asset class. Depreciation is not usually charged on
Capital WIP.

All costs incurred on building a capital asset can be
booked to an Internal Order and through the
settlement procedure can be posted onto an Asset under
construction. Subsequently on the actual readiness of
the asset for commercial production, the Asset under
construction gets capitalized to an actual asset.

75. **The company has procured 10 cars. You want to create asset masters for each car. How do you create 10 asset masters at the same time? ① ②**

> While creating the asset master there is a field on the initial create screen called number of similar assets. Update this field with 10. When you finally save this asset master you will get a pop up asking whether you want to maintain different texts for these assets. You can update different details for all 10 cars.

FI-MM-SD Integration

76. How do you go about setting the FI MM account determination? ① ②

FI MM settings are maintained in transaction code OBYC. Within this there are various transaction keys to be maintained such as BSX, WRX, GBB, PRD etc. These transactions keys are called when material movements are performed in Material Management.

For each of the transaction keys you need to select the rules for which you will be maintaining the detail. For example, transaction key BSX (for inventory balance sheet accounts).

The rules you can select are valuation modification or valuation class. Valuation modification is required if you want to maintain plant wise different GL codes.

After saving the rule you maintain the GL code for the combination of valuation modification and valuation class. For example, Transaction key GBB (offsetting account for inventory postings generally goods issue/ scrapping/delivery of goods etc)

Here you maintain the rules:

- Debit/credit
- General modification
- Valuation modification
- Valuation class

The GL account is maintained for the above combination.

77. Are the FI-MM and FI-SD account determination settings maintained at company code level? ①

No. They are at maintained at the chart of accounts level.

78. What are the additional settings required while maintaining or creating the GL codes for Inventory accounts? ①

In the Inventory GL accounts (Balance sheet) you should switch on the 'Post automatically only' tick. It is also advisable to maintain the aforesaid setting for all FI-MM accounts and FI-SD accounts. This helps in preserving the sanctity of those accounts and prevents from having any difference between FI and MM, FI and SD.

79. At what level is stock valuation possible in SAP? ① ②

The valuation in SAP can be at the plant level or the company code level. If you define valuation at the plant level then you can have different prices for the same material in the various plants. If you keep it at the company code level you can have only one price across all plants.

80. What is Valuation Class? ①

The Valuation Class in the Accounting 1 View in Material Master is the main link between the Material Master and Finance. This Valuation Class along with the combination of the transaction keys (BSX, WRX, GBB, PRD) defined above determine the GL account during posting.

We can group together different materials with similar properties by valuation class, for example, Raw material, Finished Goods, Semi Finished.

We can define the following assignments in customizing:

- ✔ All materials with same material type are assigned to just one valuation class.
- ✔ Different materials with the same material type can be assigned to different valuation classes.
- ✔ Materials with different material types are assigned to a single valuation class.

81. Can we change the valuation class in the material master once it is assigned? ① ② ③

Once a material is assigned to a valuation class in the material master record, we can change it only if the stocks for that material are nil. If stock exists for that material, then we cannot change the valuation class. In such a case, if the stock exists, you have to transfer the stock or issue the stock and make the stock nil for the specific valuation class. Only then will you be able to change the valuation class.

82. Does the moving average price change in the material master during issue of the stock, assuming that the price control for the material is Moving Average? ① ②

The moving average price in the case of goods issue remains unchanged. Goods issues are always valuated at the current moving average price. It is only in goods receipt that the moving average price might change. A goods issue only reduces the total quantity and the total value in relation to the price and the moving price remains unchanged.

83. **If the answer to the previous question is 'Yes', then list the scenario in which the moving average price of the material in the material master changes when the goods are issued. ① ②**

> The moving average price in the material master changes in the scenario of Split Valuation, which is sometimes used by organizations. If the material is subject to split valuation, the material is managed as several partial stocks and each partial stock is valuated separately.
>
> In split valuation, the material with valuation header record will have 'V' moving average price. This is where the individual stocks of a material are managed cumulatively. Here two valuation types are created, one valuation type can have 'V' (MAP) and the other valuation type can have 'S' (standard price).
>
> In this case, whenever the goods are issued from the respective valuation types, always the MAP for the valuation header changes.

84. **What is the accounting entry in the Financial books of accounts when the goods are received in unrestricted use stock? Also mention the settings to be done in the 'Automatic postings' in SAP for the specific G/L accounts. ①**

> On receipt of the goods in unrestricted-use stock, the Inventory account is debited and the GR/IR account gets credited. In customization, in the automatic postings, the Inventory G/L account is assigned to the Transaction event key BSX and the GR/IR account is assigned to the Transaction event key WRX.

85. If a material has no material code in SAP, can you default the G/L account in Purchase order or does it have to be manually entered? ① ②

If a material has no material code in SAP, we can still default the G/L account with the help of material groups. We can assign the valuation class to a material group and then in FI-automatic posting, we can assign the relevant G/L account in the Transaction event key. The assignment of a valuation class to a material group enables the system to determine different G/L accounts for the individual material groups.

86. What is the procedure in SAP for initial stock uploading? Also mention the accounting entries. ① ② ③

Initial stock uploading in SAP from the legacy system is done with inventory movement type 561(MM transaction which is performed).

✔ **Material valuated at standard price:**

For a material valuated at standard price, the initial entry of inventory data is valued on the basis of standard price in the material master. If you enter an alternative value at the time of the movement type 561, then the system posts the difference to the price difference account.

✔ **Material valuated at moving average price:**

The initial entry of inventory data is valued as follows: If you enter a value when uploading the initial data, the quantity entered is valued at this price. If you do not enter a value when entering initial data, then the quantity entered is valued at the MAP present in the material master.

✔ **The accounting entries are:**

Inventory account is debited and Inventory Historical upload account is credited.

87. How do you configure FI-SD account determination? ① ②

The FI-SD account determination happens through an access sequence. The system goes about finding accounts from more specific criteria to less specific criteria.

This is the sequence it would follow:

- ✔ It will first access and look for the combination of Customer account assignment grp/ Material account assignment grp/ Account key.

- ✔ If it does not find the accounts for the first combination it will look for Customer account assignment grp and account key combination.

- ✔ Furthermore, if it does not find accounts for the first 2 criteria's then it will look for Material account assignment grp/Account key.

- ✔ If it does not find accounts for the all earlier criteria's then finally it will look for Account key to find the GL code

Thus posting of Sales Invoices into FI are affected on the basis of a combination of Sales organization, Account type, or Customer and Material Account assignment groups and the following options are available.

- ✔ Customer AAG/Material AAG/Account type

- ✔ Material AAG/Account type

- ✔ Customer AAG/Account type

For each of theses options you can define a GL account. Thus the system uses this GL account to automatically pass the entries.

Logistics Invoice Verification

88. Can you assign multiple G/L accounts in the Purchase order for the same line item? ① ②

Yes, we can assign multiple G/L accounts in the Purchase order for the same line item. The costs can be allocated on a percentage or quantity basis. If the partial goods receipt and partial invoice receipt has already taken place, then the partial invoice amount can be distributed proportionally, i.e. evenly among the account assigned items of a Purchase order.

Alternatively the partial invoice amount can be distributed on a progressive fill-up basis, i.e. the invoiced amount is allocated to the individual account assignment items one after the other.

89. What is Credit memo and subsequent debit in Logistics Invoice verification? ① ②

The term credit memo refers to the credit memo from the vendor. Therefore posting a credit memo always leads to a debit posting on the vendor account. Credit memos are used if the quantity invoiced is higher than the quantity received or if part of the quantity was returned.

Accounting entries are: Vendor account is debited and GR/IR account is credited.

Subsequent debit: If a transaction has already been invoiced and additional costs are invoiced later, then a subsequent debit is necessary. In this case you can debit the material with additional costs, i.e. GR/IR account debit and Vendor account credit.

When entering the subsequent debit, if there is no sufficient stock coverage, only the portion for the available stock gets posted to the stock account and rest is posted to the price difference account.

90. What do you mean by Invoice parking, Invoice saving and Invoice confirmation? ① ②

✓ **Invoice parking**

Invoice Parking is a functionality that allows you to create incomplete documents and the system does not check whether the entries are balanced or not. An accounting document is not created when the invoice is in parked mode.

Thus you can create incomplete documents and then post them later to accounting when you feel they are complete. You can even rectify the Parked invoice. Many companies use this feature, as on many occasions all data relating to the invoice might not be available.

✓ **Invoice saving**

This is also called Invoice processing or Invoice posting. The accounting document gets created when the invoice is posted in SAP.

✓ **Invoice confirmation**

There is no such terminology in SAP as invoice confirmation.

91. What are Planned Delivery costs and Unplanned Delivery costs? ①

✓ **Planned Delivery costs**

Are entered at the time of Purchase order. At goods receipt, a provision is posted to the freight or customs clearing account.

For example, FRE is the account key for freight condition, hence the system can post the freight charges to the relevant freight revenue account and FR3 is the account key for Customs duty, hence the system can post the customs duty to the relevant G/L account.

These account keys are assigned to the specific condition types in the MM Pricing schema.

In terms of Invoice verification: If the freight vendor and the material vendor is the same, then we can choose the option: Goods service items + Planned delivery costs.

If the freight vendor is different from the material vendor, then for crediting only the delivery costs, we can choose the option: Planned delivery costs.

✔ **Unplanned delivery costs**
Are the costs that are not specified in the Purchase order and are only entered when you enter the invoice.

92. What is the basis on which the apportionment is done of unplanned delivery costs? ① ②

Unplanned delivery costs are either uniformly distributed among the items or posted to a separate G/L account.

For a material subject to moving average price, the unplanned delivery costs are posted to the stock account, provided sufficient stock coverage exists.

For a material subject to standard price, the unplanned delivery costs are posted to the Price difference account.

93. What Goods Receipt values will be updated if Invoice verification is done before the Goods receipt is made for the purchase order? ① ②

   Since the invoice verification has been done first the Goods Receipts will be valued with the Invoice value.

FI Month End Closing Activities

94. What are the Month End Closing Activities in FI? ① ②

- ✔ Recurring Documents.

  Create Recurring documents

  Create Batch Input for Posting Recurring Documents

  Run the Batch Input Session

- ✔ Posting Accruals or Provisions entries at month end.

- ✔ Regroup the GR/IR Account and Run the GR/IR Automatic Clearing.

- ✔ Foreign Currency Open Item Revaluation and Revalue Open Items in AR.AP.

- ✔ Maintain Exchange Rates.

- ✔ Run Balance Sheets – Run Financial Statement Version.

- ✔ Reclassify Payables and Receivables if necessary.

- ✔ Run the Depreciation Calculation.

- ✔ Fiscal Year Change of Asset Accounting if it is year end.

- ✔ Run the Bank Reconciliation.

- ✔ Open Next Accounting Period.

Controlling Module

95. Explain the organizational assignment in the controlling module? ①

Company codes are assigned to the controlling area. A controlling area is assigned to the operating concern.

Controlling Area is the umbrella under which all controlling activities of Cost Center Accounting, Product costing, Profitability Analysis and Profit Center are stored.

Operating Concern is the highest node in Profitability Analysis.

96. What is primary and secondary cost element? ①

Every Profit and Loss GL account that needs to be controlled has to be defined as a cost element in SAP. Just as in FI General Ledger Accounts exist, in Controlling we have Cost elements.

Each FI General Ledger Account that is a Profit and Loss Account is also created as a Cost element in SAP.

✔ **Primary Cost Elements**

Are those which are created from FI general Ledger Accounts and impact the financial accounts e.g. Traveling expenses, consumption account and in fact, any Profit and Loss GL account

✔ **Secondary Cost Elements**

Are those which are created only in controlling and do not affect the financials of the company. It is used for internal reporting only. The postings to these accounts do not affect the Profit or Loss of the company.

The following categories exist for secondary cost elements:

Internal Settlement:

Cost elements of this category are used to settle order costs to objects in controlling such as cost centers, pa segments etc.

Order/Results Analysis:

Used to calculate WIP on the order/project

Overheads

Used to calculate indirect costs from cost centers to orders

Assessment

Used to calculate costs during assessment

Internal Activity Allocation

Used to allocate costs during internal activity allocation such as Machine Labor etc

97. What are cost objects? ①

A cost object means a cost or a revenue collector wherein all the costs or revenues are collected for a particular cost object. Examples of this could be cost center, production order, internal order, projects, sales order

So whenever you look at any controlling function the basic thing you need to ask yourself is, "What is the cost element(expense) I want to control and what is the cost object (i.e. either the production order, sales order, internal order) I am using to control this cost element?".

Controlling is knowing the cost element and the cost object. Every time ask yourself these questions, "What is the cost element and what is the cost object?".

At the end of the period all costs or revenues in the cost object are settled to their respective receivers, which could be a GL account, a cost center, profitability analysis or an asset.

It is very important that you understand this otherwise you will struggle to understand Controlling.

90

CHAPTER 3

Controlling

Cost Center Accounting

98. How is cost center accounting linked to profit center? ①

In the master data of the Cost Center there is a provision to enter the profit center. This way all costs that flow to the cost center are also captured in the profit center.

Cost centers are basically created to capture costs e.g. admin cost center, canteen cost center etc.

Profit centers are created to capture cost and revenue for a particular plant, business unit or product line.

99. What is a cost element group? ①

Cost element group is nothing but a group of cost elements, which help one to track and control cost more effectively. You can make as many cost element groups as you feel necessary by combining various logical cost elements.

100. What is a cost center group and why is it required? ①

The cost center group is also a group of cost centers, which help one to track and control the cost of a department more effectively. You can make as many cost center groups as you feel necessary by combining various logical cost centers.

In fact you can use various combinations of cost center group with the cost element group to track and control your costs per department or across departments.

It is basically used in reporting and allocation cycles when non-consecutive cost centers are receiving costs from one sender.

101. What is the difference between Distribution and Assessment? ①

Distribution

Uses the original cost element for allocating cost to the sender cost center. Thus on the receiving cost center we can see the original cost element from the sender cost center. Distribution only allocates primary cost.

Assessment

Uses the assessment cost element category 42 to allocate cost. Thus various costs are summarized under a single assessment cost element. In the receiver cost center the original cost breakup from the sender is not available. Assessment allocates both primary as well as secondary cost.

102. Assume you want to copy a cost center plan from one year to another and there already exists some plan data in the target version for the target year. Does the copying overwrite the existing cost in the target version? ①

When you copy Plan Costs in a cost center, there is an option available to reset and overwrite the existing data or to just add the plan data into target year without overwriting the existing data.

103. What is an Activity Type? ①

Activity types classify the activities produced in the cost centers. Activity types act as cost drivers for allocating cost from cost center to other cost objects. Examples of an Activity Type could be Machine, Labor or Utilities

104. If you want to calculate the activity price through the system, what would the requirements be to do that? ① ②

In the activity type master you need to select the price indicator 1 – Plan price, automatically based on activity.

105. When activity price is calculated through system is the activity price shown as fixed or variable? ① ②

Normally when activity price is calculated through system it is shown as fixed activity price since primary costs are planned as activity independent costs.

106. What is required to be done if activity price is to be shown both fixed and variable? ① ② ③

In this case you need to plan both activity independent cost which are shown as fixed costs and activity dependent costs which are shown as variable costs.

107. Is it possible to calculate the planned activity output through system? ① ② ③

Yes. It is possible to calculate the planned activity output through system by using the Long term Planning process in the PP module.

108. Explain the process of calculating the planned activity output through Long term planning? ① ② ③

In the Long term planning process the planned production quantities are entered for the planning year in a particular scenario.

The Long term planning is executed for the scenario. This generates the planned activity requirements taking the activity quantities from the routing and multiplying with the planned production.

The activity requirements are then transferred to the controlling module as scheduled activity quantities. Thereafter you execute a plan activity reconciliation, which will reconcile the schedule activity, and the activity you have planned. The reconciliation program updates the scheduled activity quantity as the planned activity in the controlling module.

109. You want to revalue the production orders using actual activity prices. Is there a configuration setting to achieve this? ①②③

No. A month end transaction has to be run. You can revalue the production orders using actual activity prices by doing a month end transaction. You will have to follow the following menu path: Controlling-Product Costing-Month end closing-Revalue Production orders using actual activity price.

110. Where is the configuration setting to be done for carrying out revaluation of planned activity prices in various cost objects? ①②③

The configuration setting is to be done in the cost center accounting version maintenance for fiscal year. This has to be maintained for version 0. You need to select the revalue option either using own business transaction or original business transaction.

111. **At month end you calculate actual activity prices in the system. You want to revalue the production orders with the actual activity prices. What are the options available in the system for revaluation?** ① ② ③

The following options are available:

✔ You can revalue the transactions using:

Periodic price

Average price

Cumulative price

✔ Further you can revalue the various cost objects as follows:

Own business transaction - differential entries are posted

Original business transaction – the original business transaction is changed.

Internal orders

112. What is the purpose of defining internal orders? ①

Internal order is used to monitor costs for short-term events, activities. It helps in providing more information than that is provided on the cost centers. It can be widely used for various purposes.

An example would help us understand this much better.

Lets say in an organization there are various events such as trade fairs and training seminars, which are conducted during the year. These Trade fairs are organized by the marketing cost center of the organization. Therefore in this case marketing cost center is responsible for all the trade fairs costs. All these trade fairs costs are posted to the marketing cost centers. Now if the management wants an analysis of the cost incurred for each of the trade fairs organized by the marketing cost center how would the marketing manager get this piece of information across for all the trade fairs? The cost center report would not give this piece of information.

Now this is where Internal Order steps in. If you go through all cost center reports this information is not readily available since all the costs are posted to the cost center.

SAP, therefore provides the facility of using internal orders which comes in real handy in such situations. In the above scenario the controlling department would then need to create an internal order for each of the trade fairs organized.

The cost incurred for each of the trade fair will be posted to the internal orders during the month. At the month end, these costs, which are collected in the internal order, will be settled from these orders to the marketing cost center. Thus the controlling person is now in a position to analyze the cost for each of the trade fairs separately.

113. How can you default certain items while creating internal order master data? ① ②

You can do so by creating a model order and then updating the fields that you want to default in this model order. Finally attach this model order in the internal order type in the field reference order.

Once the above is done whenever you create an internal order for this order type, the field entries will get copied from the model order.

114. What is the configuration setting for the release of the internal order immediately after creation? ① ②

You have to check the "release immediately" check box in the internal order type.

Product Costing

115. What are the important Terminologies used in Product Costing? ① ②

✔ **Results Analysis Key**

This key determines how the Work in Progress is calculated.

✔ **Cost Components**

The break up of the costs that get reflected in the product costing e.g. Material Cost, Labor Cost and Overheads.

✔ **Costing Sheets**

This is used to calculate the overhead in Controlling.

✔ **Costing Variant**

For all manufactured products the price control recommended is Standard Price. To come up with this standard price for the finished good material this material has to be costed. This is done using the Costing Variant.

116. What configuration settings are maintained in the costing variant? ① ②

Costing variant forms the link between the application and Customizing, since all cost estimates are carried out and saved with reference to a costing variant. The costing variant contains all the control parameters for costing.

The configuration parameters are maintained for costing type, valuation variants, date control, and quantity structure control.

In costing type we specify which field in the material master should be updated.

In valuation variant we specify the following:

- ✔ The sequence or order the system should go about accessing prices for the material master (planned price, standard price, moving average price etc).

- ✔ It also contains which price should be considered for activity price calculation.

- ✔ How the system should select BOM and routing.

117. How does SAP go about costing a Product having multiple Bill of materials within it? ①

SAP first costs the lowest level product, arrives at the cost and then goes and costs the next highest level and finally arrives at the cost of the final product.

118. What does the concept of cost roll up mean in the product-costing context? ①

The purpose of the cost roll up is to include the cost of goods manufactured of all materials in a multilevel production structure at the topmost level of the BOM (Bill of Material)

The costs are rolled up automatically using the costing levels.

- ✔ The system first calculates the costs for the materials with the lowest costing level and assigns them to cost components.

✔ The materials in the next highest costing level (such as semi-finished materials) are then costed. The costs for the materials costed first are rolled up and become part of the material costs of the next highest level.

119. What is a settlement profile and why is it needed? ① ②

All the costs or revenues that are collected in the Production order or Sales order, for example have to be settled to a receiver at the end of the period. This receiver could be a Gl account, a cost center, profitability analysis or asset.

In order to settle the costs of the production order or sales order a settlement profile is needed.

In a settlement profile you define a range of control parameters for settlement. You must define the settlement profile before you can enter a settlement rule for a sender.

The Settlement Profile is maintained in the Order Type and defaults during creation of order.

The settlement profile includes:

✔ The retention period for the settlement documents.

✔ Valid receivers GL account, cost center, order, WBS element, fixed asset, material, profitability segment, sales order, cost objects, order items, business process.

✔ Document type is also attached here.

✔ Allocation structure and PA transfer structure is also attached to the settlement profile e.g. A1.

The settlement profile created is then attached to the order type.

120. What is Transfer or Allocation structure? ① ② ③

The Transfer structure is what helps in settling the cost from one cost object to the receiver. It is maintained in the Settlement profile defined above.

The Transfer structure has 2 parts:

- ✔ Source of cost elements you want to settle.
- ✔ Target receiver, whether it is a Profitability segment or fixed asset or cost center.

So, for settling the costs of a cost object, you need to define the transfer structure, where you mention what the costs are that you want to settle and the target receiver for that.

You fit this information in the settlement profile, which contains various other parameters, and this settlement profile is defaulted in the Order type. So every time an order is executed the relevant settlement rule is stored and at the month end, by running the transaction of the settlement of orders all the cost is passed on to the receiver.

To put in simple terms:

- ✔ You define your cost object, which could be a production order or a sales order as an example.
- ✔ You collect costs or revenues for it.
- ✔ You determine where you want to pass these costs or revenues too. For example, if the sales order is the cost object all the costs or revenues of a sales order could be passed to Profitability Analysis

121. What do you mean by a primary cost component split? ① ② ③

Primary cost split is defined when you create a cost component structure. When you switch on this setting, the primary cost from the cost center are picked up and assigned to the various cost components.

122. How do primary costs get picked up from cost center into the cost component structure? ① ② ③

This is possible when you do a plan activity price calculation from SAP. The primary cost component structure is assigned to the plan version 0 in Controlling.

123. Is it possible to configure 2 cost component structures for the same product in order to have 2 different views? ① ② ③

Yes it is possible. We create another cost component structure and assign it to the main cost component structure. This cost component structure is called the Auxiliary cost component structure that provides another view of the cost component structure.

124. How do you go about configuring sales order costing? ① ② ③

The flow is as follows:

Sales order ➜ Requirement Type ➜
Requirement Class ➜ All settings for controlling

In a sales order you have a requirement type. In configuration, the Requirement Class is attached to the requirement type and in this requirement Class all configuration settings are maintained for controlling.

In the Requirement Class we attach the costing variant; we attach the condition type EK02 where we want the sales order cost to be updated, and the account assignment category. In the account assignment category we define whether the sales order will carry cost or not. In case we do not want to carry cost on the sales order we keep the Consumption Posting field blank.

We also define here the Results Analysis version that helps to calculate the Results Analysis for the Sales order if required.

125. There are 2 plants in a company code. The first plant is the manufacturing plant and the 2nd is the selling plant. Finished goods are manufactured at the manufacturing plant and transferred to the selling plant. How is standard cost estimate calculated at the selling plant given the fact that the cost at both the plants should be the same? ①②③

The special procurement type needs to be configured which specifies in which plant the system is to look up for cost. Here a special procurement key specifying the 1st plant (manufacturing plant) should be configured.

This special procurement type must be entered in the costing view or the MRP view of the finished good material master record in the 2nd plant.

When you cost the finished good in the 2nd plant, the system will transfer the standard cost estimate from the 1st plant to the 2nd plant.

126. What is mixed costing in SAP? Give an example to explain.
①②③

Mixed costing is required when different processes are used to manufacture the same material. Mixed costing is required when you have different sources of supply for purchasing the material.

Let us take an example:

There is a finished good Xylene that can be manufactured by 3 different processes.

The first process uses an old machine and labor. The processing time is 9 hrs to manufacture.

The second process uses a semi-automatic machine and labor. The processing time is 7 hrs to manufacture.

The third process uses a fully automatic machine and the processing time is 5 hrs.

Thus cost of manufacture for the 3 processes is different. By using Mixed costing you can create a mixed price for the valuation of this finished good.

127. What configuration needs to done for using Mixed costing?
①②③

Quantity Structure type for mixed costing must be configured. Here we specify the time dependency of the structure type. The following options exist

- ✔ You have no time dependency.
- ✔ It is based on fiscal year.
- ✔ It is based on period.

This quantity structure type is then assigned to the costing version.

128. Let's say a product has three production versions. Explain the process how you would go about creating a mixed cost estimate? ① ②

The process of creating a mixed cost estimate would be as follows:

- ✔ Create procurement alternatives for each of the production version.
- ✔ Define Mixing ratios for the procurement alternatives.
- ✔ Select the configured quantity structure type and execute a material cost estimate based on the costing version.

129. What is Mixing Ratios and why are they required to be maintained before creation of cost estimate? ① ②

Mixing ratios are weighting factors assigned to the procurement alternatives. This weighting factor is obtained from the planning department based on the usage of the procurement alternatives during the planning year.

For example:

Procurement alternative 1 (production version 1) 40% will be manufactured

Procurement alternative 2 (production version 2) 35% will be manufactured

Procurement alternative 3 (production version 3) 25% will be manufactured

This % will be maintained as mixing ratios.

Thus, when the system calculates the mixed cost estimate, the system will first cost each of the production versions and then multiply each of the costs with the weighting factors.

Thus,

240 (cost of prod. Vers 1) X 40 = 9600

210 (cost of prod. Vers 2) X 35 = 7350

160 (cost of prod. Vers 3) X 25 = 4000
Mixed costs   17350/100 = 173.5

130. There are result analysis categories in WIP (Work in Process). What do you mean by the result analysis category reserves for unrealized costs? ① ② ③

If you are calculating the work in process at actual costs, the system will create reserves for unrealized costs if the credit for the production order based on goods receipts is greater than the debit of the order with actual costs incurred. The Result analysis category, RUCR (Reserves for unrealized cost), would need to be maintained. Normally this is not maintained in most of the companies.

131. Which is the Result analysis category which is normally maintained for the WIP (Work in Process) calculation? ① ②

The Result analysis category, WIPR - Work in process with requirement to capitalize costs, is normally maintained for WIP calculation.

132. Describe a by-product in SAP? ① ②

A by-product in SAP, is described as an item with a negative quantity in the Bill of Material. By-product reduces the cost of the main product. There is no Bill of Material for a by-product.

133. How do you calculate the cost of a by-product in SAP? ① ②

The by-product cost is the net realizable value. This is manually maintained in the system for the by-product through transaction code MR21 Price change.

134. How do you define a co-product in SAP? ① ② ③

A co-product (primary product or by-product) is indicated by a tick in the costing view of the material master. In the BOM all the primary products are represented as an item with negative quantity. A primary product is also indicated as a co-product in the BOM of the leading co-product. For primary products the costs are calculated using the apportionment method, while for by-products the net realizable value method applies.

135. Is it possible to use standard SAP co-product functionality in repetitive manufacturing? ① ② ③

No. It is not possible to use the standard co-product functionality in repetitive manufacturing.

136. How do you go about defining CO-Product functionality in repetitive manufacturing? ① ② ③

In repetitive manufacturing you need to use the costing BOM for the other co-product. Through arithmetical calculation you need to maintain the quantities in the costing BOM. This co-product will be shown as a negative item in the leading co-product.

137. You get an error while executing a cost estimate which says, "Item no 1 (which is a raw material) is not assigned to the cost component structure". What could be the possible root cause of the error in this scenario? ① ②

The consumption GL code for the material master is not assigned to the cost component structure. To find out how you know which GL code to assign read the next question.

138. In the above scenario how do you know which cost element is being called for? ① ②

In this case you need to the use simulation mode OMWB in MM and enter the material code plant and the movement type 261 (issue against production order). You will see the account modifier VBR and against which the GL code is available.

139. You get an error while executing a cost estimate, which says, "Item no. 1 (which is a raw material) is not assigned to the cost component structure". In this case everything is perfectly configured, what could be the possible error in this scenario? ① ②

In the material master of the raw material, the valuation class in the accounting view is incorrect.

140. Is it possible to calculate standard cost estimate for a past date? ①

No. It is not possible to calculate standard cost estimate for a past date.

141. Let's say for a particular finished good no standard cost estimate exists. Is it possible for the production people to carry on production activities like creating and releasing the production order? ① ②

Yes. It is possible to create a production order and carry out all production activities even if no standard cost estimate exists. Standard SAP allows this to happen.

142. Is it also possible to save and release the production order even if no standard cost estimate exists for the finished product? ① ②

Yes, you can do this by writing a user exit. In this case before saving the production order the system can be told to bypass the cost estimate

143. Let's say 2 production versions exist for a finished product. Which production version will the system pick up while calculating the standard cost estimate? ① ②

The system will pick up the first version by default while calculating the standard cost estimate.

144. In the previous example, lets say the product cost accountant wants the second version to be selected while creating the cost estimate. How can that be configured? ①②

There are 2 options available:

- ✔ While creating the standard cost estimate in transaction code CK11N, you can select the Production version manually or the Bill of Material and routing.

- ✔ You lock production version 1. Create a copy of production version 1 and name it as production version 3. The system will now access production version 2 as the first version.

145. What configuration is needed so that the results of the standard cost estimate are updated in fields other than the standard price? ①②③

The results of the standard cost estimate are updated in the Material Master based on the configuration done while defining Costing Type in Controlling. In this piece of configuration you specify which field in the Material Master will carry the price update once the costing run has taken place. You have a bunch of fields other than standard price in the material master which you can choose for price update.

146. What do you mean by Assembly scrap and how is it maintained in SAP? ①②③

Assembly scrap, is scrap that is expected to occur during the production of a material that is used as an assembly.

If a certain amount of scrap always occurs during the production of an assembly, the quantities and activities used must be increased by the system so that the required lot size can be produced.

To increase the lot size of an assembly you can enter a percentage, flat-rate assembly scrap in the MRP 1 view of the material master record. This assembly scrap is reflected in all the subordinate components. The system increases the quantity to be produced by the calculated scrap quantity. This increases both the materials consumed and the activities consumed and consequently the cost.

147. How are scrap costs shown in the standard cost estimate? ① ② ③

Scrap costs are assigned to the relevant cost component and can be shown separately for a material in the costed multilevel BOM.

148. How are scrap variances calculated? ① ② ③

Scrap variances are calculated by valuating the scrap quantities with the amount of the actual costs less the planned scrap costs.

149. What do you mean by Component scrap and how is it maintained in SAP? ① ② ③

Component scrap is the scrap of a material that is expected to occur during production. When an assembly is produced with this component, the system has to increase the component quantity to enable it to reach the required lot size. The component scrap can be entered in the BOM item or in the MRP 4 view of the material master.

150. What do you mean by Operation scrap and how is it maintained in SAP? ① ② ③

Operation scrap is a scrap that is expected to occur during production. Operation scrap is used to reduce the planned input quantities in follow up operations and to calculate the precise amount of assembly scrap. Operation scrap can be maintained as a % in the routing and in the BOM.

151. What are the implications if the operation scrap is maintained in the routing vs. if it is maintained in the BOM? ① ② ③

If the operation scrap is maintained only in the routing, the costing lot size is reduced by this percentage.

If the operation scrap is maintained in the BOM, the planned input (not the output quantity) is increased and any assembly scrap is reduced.

152. What is the meaning of additive costs in SAP and why is it required? ① ②

Additive costs are used to add costs manually to a material cost estimate when it cannot be calculated by the system. Examples of such costs are freight charges, insurance costs and stock transfer costs.

153. What configuration is required for additive costs? ① ②

To include additive costs in the material cost estimate you need to set the indicator "Incl. additive costs" for each valuation strategy in the valuation variant.

Furthermore you also need to set in the costing variant to include additive costs.

154. How do you configure split valuation? ① ② ③

The configuration steps involved in split valuation are as follows:

- ✔ Activate split valuation – configure whether split valuation is allowed for the company code.

- ✔ Determine the valuation categories and valuation types that are allowed for all valuation areas.

- ✔ Allocate the valuation types to the valuation categories.

- ✔ Determine the local valuation categories for each valuation area and activate the categories to be used in your valuation area.

155. What are valuation category and valuation type in split valuation? ① ② ③

In split valuation the material stock is divided according to valuation category and valuation type.

- ✔ **Valuation category**

  Determines how the partial stocks are divided according to which criteria. The following valuation categories are preset in the standard SAP R/3 system:

B	Procurement type
H	Origin type
X	Automatic batch valuation

- ✔ **Valuation type**

  Describes the characteristic of individual stock. For example:

EIGEN	In-house production (SAP standard)
FREMD	External procurement (SAP standard)

Valuation types are assigned to valuation categories.

156. What are the steps involved before you run a cost estimate for a split-valuated material? ① ② ③

- ✔ Create procurement alternatives based on the valuation types for the material.

- ✔ Maintain Mixing ratios for the procurement alternatives.

157. How do you create a material master with split valuation? ① ② ③

To create a split valuated material master proceed as follows:

- ✔ First create a valuation header record for the material. Update the Valuation category field on the accounting screen and leave the Valuation type field blank. In the Price control field, enter V (moving average price). When you save, the system creates the valuation header record.

- ✔ Then create the material for a valuation type.

  Call up the same material in creation mode again. Due to the fact that a valuation header record exists, the system requires you to enter a valuation type for the valuation category.

- ✔ Repeat step two for every valuation type planned.

158. When a standard cost estimate is run for a finished good, does SAP calculate cost estimate for its components such as raw and packing material? ① ②

Yes. SAP calculates the cost estimate even for raw and packing material and stores it in the standard price field for information purposes.

159. How do you prevent the system from calculating the cost estimate for raw and packing material when you run a standard cost estimate for the finished goods? ① ②

To prevent the system from calculating cost estimates for raw and packing material, you need to select the "No costing" checkbox in the costing view of the material master.

160. How is it possible to apply 2 different overhead rates for 2 different finished goods? ① ②

This is made possible through overhead groups. You configure 2 overhead keys. Define rates for each of these overhead keys. These two overhead keys are then assigned to the two overhead groups. These overhead groups are attached in the costing view of the finished goods material master.

Work in Progress

161. In period 1 there is a WIP posted of $22,000. In period 2 further goods issues are done to the extent of $15,000. How will the system calculate WIP for period 2? ① ②

System will post a delta WIP of $15,000 in period 2.

162. What is the basic difference in the WIP calculation for product cost by order and product cost by period (repetitive manufacturing)? ① ② ③

Generally in product cost by order, WIP is calculated at actual costs and in product cost by period WIP is calculated at target costs.

163. What are the configuration settings for calculating WIP in SAP? ① ②

- ✔ First and foremost you define secondary cost elements of type 31.

- ✔ You then define the results analysis version. This results analysis contains line ids that are nothing but the break up of costs.

- ✔ Next you define assignments. Here you assign source cost elements to the line ids defined above.

- ✔ You also define the secondary cost elements that are assigned to the line ids.

- ✔ Lastly you define the Finance GL accounts that are debited and credited when a Work in Progress is calculated.

164. How are production orders selected for calculation of WIP?

The system first runs through all production orders for the month and checks for the status of each production order. If the status of the production order is REL (Released) or PREL (Partially released) and if costs are incurred for that order, the system calculates WIP for the production order.

The system cancels the WIP for the production order when the status of the order becomes DLV (delivered) or TECO (Technically complete).

165. There is a production order with order quantity 1000 kgs. During the month 500 kgs of goods were produced. What will be the system treatment at month end? ① ②

The system will first check the status of the production order. Since the status of the order is not DLV (Delivered) it will calculate a WIP for the production order.

166. Why does the system not calculate variance for the 500 kgs that have been delivered? ① ②

In the product cost by order component the system does not calculate a variance for partially delivered stock on the production order. Whatever the balance is on the production order is considered to be WIP. In the product cost by period component, system will calculate WIP as well as variance provided.

167. Is the WIP calculated in the product cost by order component at actual costs or standard costs? ① ②

In the product cost by order component the WIP is calculated at actual costs.

168. Is the WIP calculated in the product cost by period component at actual costs or target costs? ① ②

In the product cost by period component the WIP is calculated at target costs.

Material Ledger

169. Why must you be cautious when switching on the material ledger for a plant? ① ② ③

A material ledger, once activated for a plant, cannot be switched off. Therefore it is important that the material ledger be activated carefully for a plant.

170. How do you go about configuring the material ledger? ① ②

- ✔ Activate valuation areas for material ledger.
- ✔ Assign currency types to material ledger type.
- ✔ Assign material ledger types to valuation area.
- ✔ Maintain number ranges for material ledger documents.
- ✔ Activate actual costing (whether activity update relevant for price determination).
- ✔ Activate actual cost component split.
- ✔ Customizing settings in OBYC.

171. What are the problems faced when a material ledger is activated? ① ② ③

When a material ledger is activated it is imperative that the actual costing run is done every month. The actual costing run needs to be done immediately following the new month roll over. After the actual costing run you cannot post any MM (Materials Management) entry to the previous period.

172. What are the options available while performing revaluation in an actual costing run? ① ②

- ✓ Revaluation - you can revalue the finished goods stock.

- ✓ Accrual - you can accrue the revaluation gain or loss without actually changing the price in the material master.

173. What is the configuration setting to be done for posting the accrual in the actual costing run? ① ② ③

In transaction code OBYC, select the transaction key LKW and maintain the balance sheet account for accrual.

174. What are the steps to be taken before you execute an actual costing run? ① ② ③

- ✓ Execute all the allocation cycles in the cost center accounting module.

- ✓ Execute actual activity price calculation.

- ✓ Revalue all the production orders with the actual activity prices. The under or over absorbed cost on cost centers are passed on to the production order through this step of revaluation of production orders.

- ✓ Calculate overheads, do a variance calculation and finally settle the production order.

- ✓ Finally execute the actual costing run.

175. What happens in an actual costing run? ① ②

In an actual costing run there is a process of single level price determination and multi level price determination. The production price difference variances are collected on the material ledger for each of the finished goods and semi finished goods.

During single level price determination the price difference collected on a single finished product is allocated to consumption. This allocation to the consumption is not individually allocated to the good issues.

In multi-level price determination the price difference is allocated to individual goods issues. The price differences are passed on to the next level of consumption.

The system calculates a weighted average price for the finished goods and semi finished goods. This weighted average price is called as the periodic unit price.

176. What happens when the revaluation is done in actual costing run for the previous period? ① ②

When revaluation is performed in actual costing for the previous period the price control in the material master is changed from S to V and the periodic price is updated as the valuation price for the previous period.

177. What is the importance of the price determination indicator in the material master for the purpose of the actual costing run? ① ②

There are 2 price determination indicators in the material master when the material ledger is activated.

They are as follows:

2　Transaction based.

3　Single level / multi level.

In the case of a material master record having a price determination indicator of 2, no actual costing will take place. In the case of a material master having a price determination indicator of 3, actual costing will take place.

178. What should be the price control for a material master that has a price determination indicator 3 where material ledger is activated? ① ② ③

In such a case only price control S is possible where the price determination 3 is activated in material master.

Profitability Analysis

179. Explain the organizational assignment in the PA module? ①

The operating concern is the highest node in Profitability Analysis. The operating concern is assigned to the Controlling Area.

All Profitability Analysis transactions are stored within the operating concern. The operating concern is nothing more than a nomenclature for defining the highest node in PA.

180. What is the functionality of the PA module? ①

PA module is the most important module when it comes to analyzing the results of the organization.

In this module you basically collect the revenues from the sale order, the costs from the production order, cost center or internal order and analyze their results.

The interesting part about this module is that when it collects the costs and revenues it also collects the characteristics associated with the costs and revenues.

So, for example, using the PA module you can find out the following:

- ✔ Profit of a certain product.
- ✔ Profit of a certain product in a certain region.
- ✔ Profit of a certain product in a certain region by a certain customer.
- ✔ Profit of a certain product in a certain region by a certain sales person.

And the list can go on in depth.

181. How are characteristics defined in the Profitability analysis module? ① ②

Several essential characteristics (sales organization, customer, product etc.) are predefined automatically for every operating concern. These are known as fixed characteristics. In addition to fixed characteristics up to 50 non-fixed characteristics can be added to an operating concern. These non-fixed characteristics must be added to the field catalog before they can be used to define a new operating concern.

182. What are Characteristics and Value Fields? ①

In the operating concern two things are basically defined:

✔ **Characteristics**

Characteristics are those aspects that we want to break down the profit logically into things such as customer, region product, product hierarchy, sales person.

✔ **Value Fields**

Value Fields are the values associated with these characteristics. For example, sales, raw material cost, labor cost, overheads.

Once you define the characteristics and value fields these values are updated in the table.

183. Where do the characteristics in Profitability Analysis come from? ①

The characteristics, that are defined above, basically come from either the Customer Master or the Material Master.

184. How do various values (revenues and costs) flow into PA? ①

The sales revenue comes from the condition type in SD. We need to map the condition type in SD, to the respective value fields in customizing, to have the revenue flow into PA.

The cost comes from cost estimates, which are transferred using the PA transfer structure, which we covered in the product costing section.

The various cost components of the cost component structure are assigned to the value field of PA module and this is how the costs come into PA.

Once the actual revenue and the standard cost defined above are captured in PA the variances are also transferred into PA.

This way the standard cost variances equal the actual cost. So actual revenue - actual cost helps to determine the profit.

185. How do you configure the assignment of variances from product costing to the COPA module? ① ②

The variance categories from product costing along with the cost element are assigned to the value fields in COPA.

186. Once you have captured all the costs and revenues how do you analyze them? ① ②

The costs and revenues, which we have captured in the above manner, are then analyzed by writing reports using the Report Painter Functionality in SAP.

187. What is characteristic Derivation in the Profitability Analysis Module? ①②

Characteristic Derivation is usually used when you want to derive the characteristics. An example - you want to derive the first two characteristics of the product hierarchy.

In such cases you define characteristic derivation where you maintain the rules, which contain the table names of the product hierarchy fields and the number of characters to be extracted, and it also specifies the target characteristic field in PA.

188. What is the basic difference in customizing in Profitability analysis as compared to other modules? ①②③

In PA when we configure the system i.e. creating operating concern, maintain structures, no customizing request is generated. The configuration needs to be transported through a different transaction called KE3I.

189. What is the difference between Account based Profitability Analysis and Costing based Profitability Analysis? ①②③

Account based profitability analysis is a form of profitability analysis (PA) that uses accounts as its base and has an account-based approach. It uses costs and revenue elements.

Costing based profitability analysis is a form of profitability analysis that groups costs and revenues according to value fields and costing based valuation approaches. The cost and revenues are shown in value fields.

190. What are the advantages and disadvantages of account based profitability analysis versus costing based profitability analysis? ① ② ③

The advantage of account based PA is that it is permanently reconciled with financial accounting.

The disadvantages are that it is not as powerful as the costing based PA, since it uses accounts to get values. No contribution margin planning can be done since it cannot access the standard cost estimate. Furthermore no variance analysis is readily available.

The advantages of the costing based PA are plentiful:
- Greater Reporting capabilities since many characteristics are available for analysis.
- This form of PA accesses the Standard cost estimate of the manufactured product and gives a split according to the cost component split (from the product costing module) when the bills are posted.
- Contribution margin can be planned in this module since the system automatically accesses the standard cost estimate of the product based on the valuation approaches.
- Variance analysis is ready available here since the variance categories can be individually mapped to the value fields.

Disadvantages:
- Since it uses a costing based approach, it does not sometime reconcile with financial accounting.

191. Can both Account based and Costing based Profitability analysis be configured at the same time? ① ② ③

Yes. It is possible to configure both types of costing based profitability analysis at the same time.

192. What is the advantage of configuring both the type of Profitability analysis together? ① ② ③

The advantage of activating account based profitability analysis along with costing based PA is that you can easily reconcile costing based profitability analysis to account based profitability analysis, which means indirectly reconciling with Financial accounting.

193. Is there any additional configuration required for Account based profitability analysis as compared to costing based profitability analysis? ① ② ③

No. There are no special configurations required except for activating the account based profitability analysis while maintaining the operating concern.

194. What is the difference between Profitability analysis and Profit center accounting? ①

Profitability analysis lets you analyze the profitability of segments of your market according to products, customers, regions and divisions. It provides your sales & marketing and planning & management organizations with decision support from a market oriented viewpoint.

Profit center accounting lets you analyze profit and loss for profit centers. It makes it possible to evaluate different areas or units within your company. Profit center can be structured according to region, plants, functions or products (product ranges).

195. What configuration settings are available to set up valuation using material cost estimate in costing based profitability analysis? ① ②

In costing based profitability analysis you define costing keys. A costing key is a set of access parameters, which are used in valuation to determine which data in Product cost planning should be read. In the costing key you attach the costing variant.

In the costing key you specify whether the system should read the current standard cost estimate, the previous standard cost estimate or the future standard cost estimate or a saved cost estimate.

The configuration settings to determine this costing key areas follows:

✔ Assign costing keys to the products – three costing keys can be attached to a single product for a specific point of valuation, record type and plan version.

✔ Assign costing keys to Material types.

✔ Assign costing keys to any characteristics – you can use your own strategy to determine the costing keys. This is through user defined assignment tables.

Profit Center

196. What is the basic purpose of creating a Profit Center? ①

The basic purpose of creating a profit center is to analyze the revenues and costs for a particular product line, or a plant or a business unit. Even though you can generate balance sheets and profit & loss accounts per Profit Center, a profit center should basically be used as a tool for internal reporting purposes only.

If you legally have to produce the balance sheets and profit & loss accounts for a profit center then it is advisable to create it as a company code instead of as a profit center

197. How does the cost and revenue flow to the Profit Center? ①

The profit center is stored in the cost center. This way the costs flow to the profit center.

The profit center is also stored in the material master. This way all sales orders created for the finished product, automatically pick up the profit center from the material master and all the revenues and costs coming from this sales order, for that finished product, are passed on to this profit center.

A profit center document is created in addition to the finance document whenever revenue or consumption takes place. This document contains the details of the profit center.

Once both the costs and revenues flow to the profit center you can write reports using the Report Painter to get intelligent analysis. You can also use SAP standard reports.

198. Statistical key figures are created in the cost center accounting module. Now the same statistical key figures are required in the profit center accounting module. Is it required to maintain the statistical key figure in the PCA module? ① ②

No, because the statistical key figures are created in a controlling area. Profit center is a sub module within controlling area. The statistical key figure is created for the controlling area and as such is available in the profit center accounting module.

199. What are the precautions to be taken while maintaining the 3KEH table for profit center accounting? ① ②

You should not maintain the customer and vendor reconciliation accounts in the 3KEH table. Furthermore, you should also not maintain the special GL accounts in this table because we are transferring the customer and vendor balances to profit center module through separate month end programs. If the reconciliation's accounts are maintained here it will result in double posting in the profit center module.

200. Should secondary cost elements be maintained in the 3KEH table? ① ②

No. Here we maintain only those accounts for which the value should flow from FI to PCA. Secondary cost elements are already defined in the controlling module, which will also reflect in the postings in PCA.

201. How can the default settings be maintained for cost elements per company code? ① ②

The default settings can be maintained in transaction OKB9. Here we can specify for a company code, cost element, which is the cost center to be defaulted, or whether profitability segment is to be automatically derived. Furthermore we can also maintain whether business area is mandatory or profit center is mandatory and can maintain the default business areas and profit centers.

202. What are the other important activities in Profit Center? ①

The assignments of profit center to the cost center and also assignment of profit center to the material master is what will determine the success of the Profit center posting. If these assignments are wrongly done then the profit center postings will not come in properly.

Period End Closing Activities in Controlling

203. What are the period end closing activities in controlling? ①

The following are the period end closing activities in Controlling:

✓ Repost CO Documents that were incorrectly posted.

✓ Run Distribution or Assessment Cycles.

✓ Assess cost center costs to Profitability analysis module.

✓ Run the Overhead Calculation in Product Costing.

✓ Run the WIP Calculation in Product Costing.

✓ Run the Variance Calculation in Product Costing.

✓ Run the Settlement Calculation in Product Costing, which will post all the WIP and variance to Finance and PA.

✓ Transfer Balance Sheet Items like Receivables and Payables.

✓ Run Results Analysis for Sales Order if applicable.

✓ Run Settlement of Sales Orders to PA.

General Questions

204. What is the FICO organizational set up on your current project?

Example:

There is a single operating concern. One controlling area is attached to the operating concern. All the company codes of the group are attached to the same controlling area. All the company codes use the same chart of accounts.

Notes

Notes

Notes

OTHER BOOKS FROM GENIE PRESS

http://www.geniepress.com

---

201 Interview Questions
SAP Business Information Warehouse

by Raj Mani Thiyagarajan

Raj is a SAP Certified BW consultant with many years of SAP BW teaching, consulting and interviewing candidates. His articles have been published in leading BW and SAP magazines. Raj holds a BSc degree in Electrical Engineering and is currently a partner in a leading ERP consulting company.

144

Printed in the United States
75635LV00001B/51-64